Options Wheel Strategy

How to Generate an Income Stream Using Cash Secured Puts and Covered Calls

Table of Contents

Introduction

Imagine yourself 10 years from now. You're likely seeing yourself island hopping, building a family, or pursuing your passion. No one dreams of sitting at a desk, working a 9-to-5 every day of their lives. Having a job is one way to secure a stable stream of monthly income. However, you'll never grow your wealth or live your dream life if you rely on your salary alone. If the average millionaire has around 7 income streams, then you need 5 to lead the life you want. Trading options can be one of them.

The Options Wheel strategy will transform the way you approach investments and trading. This book will be your guide on your journey toward financial growth. It will teach you everything you need to know without overwhelming you with jargon and complicated techniques. It is ideal for ambitious beginners who wish to set reasonable expectations and get a deep understanding of the strategies they can use to reshape their financial future.

While this book is easy to follow and understand, it offers a comprehensive exploration of the Options Wheel strategy. It explains how this strategy aligns with your goals of obtaining consistent income streams, covers the basics of the strategy, and teaches you how to master cash-secured puts and covered calls. You'll find a step-by-step guide on how to implement the Options Wheels strategy and how to put advanced techniques into use. All the concepts in the book are broken down into manageable sections and supported by real-world examples.

Once you reach the end of this book, you'll be ready to put all the knowledge you've learned into practice. Whether you dream of implementing your retirement plan, growing your portfolio, feeding your curiosity, or pursuing your ambitions, this book will be your ticket to financial success.

Chapter 1:

Understanding the Options Wheel Strategy

This chapter delves into the basics of options trading and explains key terms you must be familiar with before diving into the stock market. You'll learn about the benefits and risks of trading options and understand the rationale behind the Options Wheel Strategy. Reading this chapter, you'll discover this strategy and its role in the financial markets. You'll explore how this strategy aligns with the goals of investors who seek consistent income streams and concepts that traders should keep in mind.

The Basics of Options Trading

When you trade options, you can gain insight into where the general stock market or certain securities are headed. You'll be able to assess whether the market value of the securities you're interested in will head up or down in the future and if it's a good time to buy and sell. An Option is a contract. It allows a trader to invest in and even sell an underlying asset by a certain date at a set cost. When using options to determine if the price will go up or down, you don't need to buy the asset.

There are a few terms that you need to understand to better understand the concept of options trading:

- **Call option:** allows you to buy a security at a set price by a specified date.

- **Put option:** allows you to sell a security at a future price and date.

- **Premium:** the price of purchasing a premium and is calculated based on the underlying asset's value.

- **Strike price:** the price at which you can buy an underlying stock for call options and sell shares for put options.

- **Expiration date:** each option contract has an expiration date before which traders must exercise at the strike price.

- **Derivative:** options are known as a derivative because they "derive" their value from underlying assets.

- **In-the-money/out-of-the-money:** the expiration date and the price of the underlying security determine whether an option is profitable (in-the-money), or not (out-of-the-money).

- **Intrinsic value:** underlying asset's stock price - option contract's strike price.

- **Extrinsic value:** other factors affecting the premium, such as how far the expiration date is.

Pricing

Say the current price of a stock is $50 a share. You'll have different premiums for different option contracts, depending on the strike prices. For instance, if the strike price is $40, this would be the highest call option premium and the lowest put option premium. At a $60 strike price, this would be the lowest call option premium and the highest put option premium. There can also be other strike prices, such as $45 and $55, between the highest and lowest option premiums.

The first thing you'd do when trading options is pay the premium. This gives you the option to buy the stock (call options) or sell it (put options) at the set strike price by the specified expiration date. Call options with lower strike prices have higher intrinsic values because traders would buy the stock at a price lower than its current market price. If the stock price remains $50, your call options would be in-the-money, and you should go ahead and buy it at a discount.

In retrospect, put options with a higher strike price have higher intrinsic values because traders would be selling the stock at a price that's higher than its current market price. Your put options would also be in-the-money if the stock price remains $5o. However, you'd be able to sell it at a higher price, such as $60.

Trading

You can implement numerous options trading strategies, ranging from simple and straightforward ones to intricate and more complex approaches. All trades generally follow the same goal: call options are how traders put money on rising values, and put options are how they bet on falling ones.

An options contract gives the trader the opportunity to buy or sell at least 100 shares of securities without the obligation to exercise call or put options in case the trade is out of the money. In this case, the trader will lose the premium they initially paid for the contract. While this might be a loss, it's still a low-cost and low-risk way to gain insight into various asset classes without committing to anything.

By trading options, you'll determine whether an asset's value will rise or fall in the future, estimate the amount by which it will rise or fall, and approximate the date by which this fluctuation will take place. When trading, you'll want the asset's price to either rise or fall to reach the break-even point (the premium you paid + the strike price).

Call options: you want the underlying asset's price to rise above its break-even or price. This way, you can close your position by selling the option. You'll earn the difference between the premium that you originally paid and the current price you sold for. You can also buy the underlying asset at the predetermined strike price.

Put options: you can buy the contract once the asset's price falls below the break-even price. You'll then close your position by selling the contract and eating the difference between what you paid and the current market price. You can also sell the underlying asset at the predetermined strike price.

You can let the contract expire if you find that the trade won't be profitable. In that case, you'll only lose what you paid for the option contract, which is usually the premium price and additional trading fees.

What Is the Options Wheel Strategy?

The Options Wheel Strategy is also widely known as the triple income strategy. This technique allows you to generate consistent income while trading options alongside stocks, making it superior to the popular buy-and-hold strategy. The Wheel Options Strategy is bullish, which means that to make money, you need to go for a stock that you expect to go higher. It includes the cash-secured put, which means that you sell a put option and keep the money for the stock aside to buy it if it's assigned. This way, you might either get it for less than its market value or keep the selling premium in case it's not assigned. You are obliged to buy 100 shares at the strike price, which is a discount price, of the put option you sold, receiving a premium in return. For example, if the strike price for a put option is $40, you'd have to have $4,000 readily available in your trading account to cover the price of 100 shares.

The strategy also includes covered call, which means you'd have an amount of security equivalent to the value of the call options you wish to sell. To do that, you'd sell call options on an asset in which you hold a long position, allowing you to generate earnings. When you sell a covered call, you'll get a premium for the shares you sold rather than selling them directly on the stock market. You have to sell a call option for every 100 shares of the stock you own, which means that you'd sell 4 calls if you own 400 shares of a certain stock. A covered call is a great way to diversify your investment portfolio because it serves as a hedge. It generates income even when the stocks go down or maintain their market price.

When using this strategy, you'd continuously sell cash-secured puts until they're assigned. Then, you'd sell covered calls against these assigned shares. Once the covered calls are assigned as well, you'd repeat the cycle by selling other cash-secured puts, hence the term "wheel strategy." Traders that implement this strategy generally have 3 income-generating sources: puts, calls, and long-term stocks.

Characteristics

- **This Is a Long Theta Trading Approach**

One of the main reasons many experienced traders prefer to implement the Options Wheels Strategy is that it benefits from time decay. Theta refers to the rate at which the price of an option will decline or decay over time. When you buy an option, you want the underlying stock to move in a higher direction to make the option you have more valuable. However, the clock isn't in your favor because the value of the option declines over time.

When you sell an option, you collect a premium from the buyer. So if you're selling a put, you are willing to buy. If you're selling a call, you are willing to sell the underlying stock at a certain price if the buyer decides to exercise the option.

When you sell a put, you'll benefit from time decay as long as the underlying stock's price doesn't fall dramatically. If it's relatively stable or increases, the put option you sold will lose value over time. You can then repurchase it at a lower price and keep the difference as profit.

- **Neutral to Slightly Bullish Market Outlook**

Using this strategy, you will earn profit even if the market remains flat. A generally neutral market, or one that gradually moves upward, is the ideal trading environment for this approach. On the other hand, you will likely lose money if the market environment is fast-moving.

Selling a put option means you're putting your money on the belief that the underlying stock's price won't fall dramatically. If the option gets assigned, selling covered calls means that you're betting that the price won't rise significantly. That is why it's best to implement this strategy if you see slow and gradual changes in the market.

What You Need to Know before Using This Strategy

Choose Your Stocks Carefully

Don't trade a stock unless you're willing to hold it forever. High option premiums aren't the only thing to consider when choosing stocks to trade. If you choose a stock for this reason only, you might want to sell it at a loss if you notice that the stock price is falling. Volatility, business fundamentals, diversification, and liquidity are among the numerous factors you need to consider when looking at stock options to trade. If you don't wish to choose individual stocks, you can apply the Options Wheel Strategy to ETFs instead.

Don't Lose Track of Your Cost Basis

When you're selling options, you will collect several option premiums. That is why you need to keep track of all of them. Whenever you're assigned shares, subtract all the option premiums you collected from the cost basis.

For instance, say you sell a put option with a $100 strike price. You then receive a $0.5 premium for each share. Since the contract represents 100 shares, the total premium will be $50.

When the stock price falls, and the buyer exercises the option, you will be assigned to buy 100 shares of stock at the $100 strike price. Since you received a premium of $0.5 per share, however, you'll need to calculate your cost basis by subtracting the premium from the strike price (100 - 0.5). Your cost basis or actual cost per share will be $99.5.

Consider Your Cost Basis When Selling Covered Calls

Only sell covered calls when they are above, or at least break even with your cost basis. Selling a $95 strike call option when your cost basis is $99.5 puts you at risk of selling the stock at a loss. You should consider holding if the stock's current market price is a lot lower than what you bought the shares for. You might have to take the loss if the price doesn't go higher in the near future and you don't want to hold the stock any longer.

While the Options Wheel Strategy looks promising and easy in theory, you shouldn't jump the gun. Any trading strategy or approach has its pros and cons, and one of the downsides of this strategy is that you have to be very mindful when trading stocks that are rapidly increasing in value. In this case, you'll make more profit if you hold 100 shares of stock instead of starting the wheel. Conversely, if a stock falls significantly after you get assigned, you won't be able to sell covered calls at the break-even point or above your cost basis. You have to account for volatility because this factor determines the price that options trade for.

Chapter 2:

Mastering Cash Secured Puts

In options trading, investors have the opportunity to engage in various strategies that allow them to profit from market movements, manage risk, or generate income. One such strategy is the cash-secured put. It involves selling put options while having enough cash reserves to cover the potential obligation of buying the underlying asset.

Here's a break down of the key components of this strategy:

Put Options: This is a financial contract that doesn't give an obligation but gives the right to the holder to sell a certain underlying asset at a pre-decided cost (the strike price) on a specific expiration date. Put options are typically used by investors as a form of insurance against a potential drop in the price of the underlying asset.

Selling Put Options: When an investor engages in a cash-secured put strategy, they sell put options to other market participants. By selling a put option, the investor agrees to potentially buy the underlying asset from the option holder if the option holder decides to exercise their right to sell.

Cash Reserves: The term "cash-secured" refers to the fact that the investor needs to have enough cash in their account to cover the potential obligation of buying the underlying asset at the strike price if the option holder exercises the put option. This cash serves as collateral to secure the trade. The amount of cash required is determined by the number of contracts sold and the strike price of the options.

Income Generation: Investors who sell cash-secured puts do so with the goal of generating income. They receive a premium (a fee) from the buyer of the put option upfront. This premium is the investor's compensation for taking on the obligation to potentially buy the underlying asset at a predetermined price.

Outcomes: There are a few potential outcomes for a cash-secured put strategy:

If the cost of the underlying asset stays above the price of the strike until the option expires, it will probably be worthless by the time it expires, and the investor will get to keep the premium as profit.

If the underlying asset's price drops significantly below the strike price, the put option holder may exercise their right to sell the asset at the strike price. In this case, the investor must purchase the asset at the strike price, using the cash reserves they set aside.

If the underlying asset's price drops moderately, the investor may choose to close the position by buying back the put option at a lower price before expiration.

It's important to note that while cash-secured puts can be a strategy for income generation and potential capital appreciation, they still carry risks. Market fluctuations can lead to potential losses, and investors should be well-informed about the strategy and its potential outcomes before engaging in options trading. Additionally, the strategy requires careful consideration of the specific underlying asset, strike price, expiration date, and overall market conditions. As with any investment strategy, individuals should conduct thorough research and consider consulting with financial professionals before implementing cash-secured puts or any other options trading strategy.

Executing Cash Secured Puts Effectively

This involves a series of steps with various factors to consider in order to optimize your strategy. Here's a step-by-step guide:

Understand the Basics

Before diving into cash-secured puts, make sure you have a solid understanding of options, including terminology, rights, obligations, and risks associated with different strategies.

Selecting Suitable Stocks

When selecting stocks for a cash-secured put strategy, consider the following factors:

Market Trends: Choose stocks that are generally stable or have a bullish outlook. Stocks with consistent uptrends are preferable as they are less likely to experience significant drops.

Implied Volatility: Implied volatility reflects the market's expectation of a stock's future price fluctuations. Higher implied volatility generally leads to higher option premiums. Look for stocks with moderate to higher implied volatility to generate more substantial premiums.

Sector Performance: Consider stocks from sectors that are performing well and have positive growth prospects. Avoid ones that are highly volatile or undergoing major shifts.

Conduct Fundamental Analysis

Evaluate the fundamentals of the stocks you're considering. Look at earnings reports, revenue growth, debt levels, and other financial metrics to gauge the overall health of the company.

Technical Analysis

Use technical analysis to understand the stock's price movements, support and resistance levels, and potential entry points. This can help you choose appropriate strike prices and expiration dates.

Identify Strike Price and Expiration Date

Choose a strike price that is slightly below the current market price of the stock. This allows you to capitalize on the premium while potentially getting the stock at a discount if the option is exercised. Select an expiration date that aligns with your investment timeframe and market outlook.

Calculate Potential Return and Risk

Estimate the potential return on investment (ROI) and understand the risk involved. Calculate the potential return as the premium you receive divided by the cash you need to set aside to cover the obligation of buying the stock at the strike price.

Set Aside Cash Reserves

Make sure you have enough cash in your account to cover the potential obligation of buying the stock at the strike price. The cash will act as collateral and is crucial for executing a cash-secured put.

Place the Trade

Use your chosen trading platform to execute the cash-secured put trade. You'll sell the put option and receive the premium. Make sure to review all the trade details before confirming.

Monitor and Manage

Once the trade is executed, monitor the market closely. If the stock price remains above the strike price and the option expires, you keep the premium as profit. If the stock price drops significantly, be prepared to potentially buy the stock at the strike price if the option is exercised.

Adapt to Changing Conditions

Market conditions can change, affecting the performance of the stock and the option. Be ready to adjust your strategy if needed, including rolling the option to a different expiration date or taking other protective measures.

Continuous Learning

Options trading and strategies like cash-secured puts require ongoing learning and adaptation. Stay informed about market trends, economic news, and changes in the companies you're trading.

Understanding the obligations and risks associated with selling puts is essential for anyone considering options trading, particularly the cash-secured put strategy. Selling puts involves potential obligations that could result in financial consequences, so it's crucial to be fully aware of these aspects and have a robust risk management plan in place.

Importance of Understanding Obligations

Obligation to Buy Stock: When you sell a put option, you're obligated to buy the underlying stock at the strike price if the option holder chooses to exercise the option. This obligation comes with a potential financial commitment, so you need to be prepared to fulfill it.

Market Risk: The stock price can move against your favor, resulting in a scenario where the stock's market price is significantly lower than the strike price. In this case, you might end up buying the stock at a higher price than its market value.

Time Sensitivity: Options have expiration dates. If the stock price drops close to the strike price and the option approaches expiration, you might face a decision to either buy the stock at a potentially inflated price or close the position at a loss.

Practical Methods of Risk Management

Position Sizing: Determine the appropriate position size based on your risk tolerance. Avoid committing a significant portion of your capital to a single trade. Consider diversifying your options trades across different stocks or strategies.

Select Strike Prices Wisely: Choose strike prices that reasonably balance premium income and the potential obligation to buy the stock. Strike prices that are too close to the current market price might expose you to higher risk.

Set Stop-Losses: Consider implementing stop-loss orders to limit potential losses. If the stock price drops significantly, triggering the stop-loss, you can exit the position before you lose too much.

Rolling Options: If the stock price moves unfavorably but hasn't reached the strike price, consider rolling the option to a later expiration date. This extends your timeframe and might give the stock more time to recover.

Monitoring and Adjusting: Regularly monitor the performance of your options positions. If the market conditions or the stock's outlook changes significantly, be ready to adjust or close the position to limit potential losses.

Maintain Adequate Cash Reserves: Always make sure you have enough cash in your account to cover the potential obligation of buying the stock. This is the fundamental principle of the cash-secured put strategy.

Risk-Reward Ratio: Assess the potential return on investment against the potential risk. A favorable risk-reward ratio means the potential reward justifies the potential risk.

Education and Research: Continuously educate yourself about options trading, market trends, and economic indicators. Being well-informed helps you make more informed decisions.

Practice with Paper Trading: If you're new to options, consider practicing with paper trading (simulated trading) to gain experience without risking real capital.

Consult Professionals: If you're unsure about any aspect of options trading or risk management, seek advice from financial advisors or professionals who specialize in options.

Remember that options trading carries inherent risks, and no strategy can completely eliminate the possibility of losses. Risk management is about minimizing potential losses while maximizing potential gains. Be disciplined, patient, and cautious as you execute your options trading strategies.

Exit Strategies

Exit strategies and adjustments are crucial aspects of managing cash-secured put positions, especially when those positions are at risk of being assigned. Being proactive in managing your positions can help you navigate potential assignment scenarios and minimize potential losses. Here are insights into exit strategies, adjustments, and techniques for managing positions that might lead to assignment:

Close the Position Early

If the market moves against your position and the stock price approaches or drops below the strike price, consider closing the position before the expiration. This can help you avoid potential assignments and limit your losses.

Roll the Option

If the stock price is nearing the strike price and you still believe in its long-term prospects, you can consider rolling the option to a later date with a similar or adjusted strike price. This gives the stock more time to recover and reduces the risk of assignment.

Adjust the Strike Price

If you're concerned about potential assignment but still want to stay in the trade, consider adjusting the strike price downward. This might lower the potential obligation to buy the stock but will also likely result in a lower premium.

Use Vertical Spreads

Instead of selling a naked put, you can use a vertical put spread strategy. This involves simultaneously selling a put option and buying a put option at a lower strike price. The bought put acts as a hedge against potential assignment.

Hedge with Stock Ownership

If you're assigned the stock and still believe in its long-term potential, you can turn the situation into a covered call strategy. This involves selling call options on the stock you now own. The premium from the calls can offset potential losses.

Assess the Company's Fundamentals

Before and during the trade, continually assess the company's fundamentals. If negative news or changes in the company's financial health emerge, it might be prudent to exit the trade early to avoid potential assignment.

Be Mindful of Dividend Dates

If the stock pays dividends and you're holding a short put position around the dividend expiration date, you might get assigned early to allow the holder to capture the dividend. Be aware of such scenarios and adjust your strategy accordingly.

Have a Plan for Assignment

In the event of assignment, be ready with a plan to manage the stock you acquire. Decide beforehand whether you're comfortable holding the stock long-term, selling covered calls against it, or selling it immediately.

Regularly Review and Adjust

Markets change, and so do companies' prospects. Regularly review your positions and adjust your strategy based on new information and changing conditions.

Paper Trading and Backtesting

Before implementing any adjustment strategy, practice with paper trading or backtesting to understand how different adjustments might impact your position under various market scenarios.

Stay Calm and Disciplined

Market volatility can lead to emotional decisions. Stay disciplined, avoid knee-jerk reactions, and base your decisions on sound analysis and risk management principles.

Exploring Advanced Strategies

Rolling options is an advanced strategy that involves closing an existing options position and simultaneously opening a new position with different parameters, such as a different strike price or expiration date. This technique is employed to manage or adjust a position that isn't performing as expected or to extend the trade's duration. In the context of cash-secured puts, rolling options can be used to enhance income and potentially turn losing positions into winning ones. Here's how rolling options can be employed to enhance income:

Rolling to a Later Expiration Date

If the stock's price is moving against your position, but you still have faith in its long-term prospects, you can roll the option to a later expiration date. This gives the stock more time to potentially recover while allowing you to collect additional premium by selling another put option. The premium received from the new option can help offset potential losses from the original position.

Rolling to a Lower Strike Price

If the stock price has dropped significantly and is close to or below the strike price of your original put option, consider rolling the option to a lower strike price. This can allow you to collect a higher premium for the new put option, which can help improve your overall income potential.

Rolling Upward for Bullish Reversals

If the stock price has shown signs of reversing its down-trend and becoming bullish, you might roll the option to a higher strike price. This can allow you to capture more premium and potentially participate in the stock's upward movement while still maintaining the cash-secured put strategy.

Using Credit Spreads

Rolling options can also involve transitioning to more complex strategies like credit spreads. A credit spread involves simultaneously selling one option and buying another option of the same type (either both puts or both calls). This can mitigate potential losses and enhance income through the net premium received from the spread.

Adjusting Deltas and Risk Profiles

By rolling options, you can adjust your position's overall delta (the measure of the position's sensitivity to stock price changes). This can align your position with your market outlook and risk tolerance.

Continuous Premium Collection

Rolling options allows you to continue collecting premium income, which can be particularly advantageous if the stock's price remains range-bound or if you expect increased volatility.

Consider Commissions and Fees

Keep in mind that rolling options involves multiple transactions, which can result in additional commissions and fees. Make sure to factor these costs into your decision-making process.

Monitor Market Conditions

Before rolling options, carefully evaluate the current market conditions, company news, and overall economic outlook. Your decision to roll should be based on a well-informed analysis.

Chapter 3:

Mastering Covered Calls

Covered calls are a powerful tool in generating income, and they play a key role in the Options Wheel strategy. This strategy is a systematic approach that involves selling cash-secured puts and, if assigned, converting the resulting stock positions into covered calls.

Covered Calls

A covered call is an options strategy where an investor holds a long position in a stock and simultaneously sells a call option on that same stock. The call option seller (also known as the writer) receives a premium upfront in exchange for agreeing to sell their shares of the underlying stock at a predetermined price (the strike price) if the option buyer decides to exercise the option before or on the expiration date.

Options Wheel Strategy

The Options Wheel strategy combines two primary components: selling cash-secured puts and utilizing covered calls.

Selling Cash-Secured Puts: In the first step of the strategy, investors sell cash-secured put options. This involves selling put options while maintaining enough cash in the trading account to cover the potential obligation of buying the underlying stock at the strike price. The goal is to collect premium income from the put sales and potentially acquire the stock at a discount if the put options are assigned due to a drop in price.

Conversion to Covered Calls: If the put options are assigned, and the investor acquires the underlying stock, the strategy transitions to the covered call phase. At this point, the investor holds the stock and can then sell covered call options on those shares. By selling covered calls, the investor generates additional income from the premiums received while still retaining ownership of the stock.

Benefits of Covered Calls in the Options Wheel

Income Generation: Covered calls allow investors to generate consistent income through the premium received from selling the call options. This income can provide a steady stream of cash flow.

Enhanced Returns: By selling covered calls on stocks they already own, investors can potentially enhance their overall returns, especially in neutral or slightly bullish market conditions.

Reduced Cost Basis: If the stock was initially acquired through the cash-secured put strategy, selling covered calls can further reduce the effective cost basis of the stock. This means the investor effectively buys the stock at an even lower net price.

Risk Mitigation: The premium received from selling covered calls provides a buffer against potential losses in the stock's price. If the stock price drops, the call option premium can offset the decline.

Flexibility: Covered calls can be tailored to align with an investor's risk tolerance and market outlook. Varying expiration dates and strike prices offer several risk profiles and income potential.

Use in Different Market Conditions: Covered calls can be effective in neutral to slightly bullish market environments, making them versatile tools for income generation in a range of scenarios.

Covered calls can be implemented using different strategies that cater to various market conditions and investor preferences. Here's a guide to several covered call strategies, along with their benefits, drawbacks, and suitability for different market conditions:

Basic Covered Call

- **Benefits:** Simple and easy to understand. Generates premium income while retaining stock ownership.

- **Drawbacks:** Limited potential for capital appreciation if the stock price rises significantly.

- **Suitability:** Suitable for neutral to slightly bullish market conditions. Good for conservative investors seeking income without excessive risk.

Out-of-the-Money (OTM) Covered Call

- **Benefits:** Provides more upside potential as the call option is sold at a higher strike price. Higher premium income compared to in-the-money options.

- **Drawbacks:** Lower downside protection compared to in-the-money options. Might lead to missed capital gains if the stock price increases significantly.

- **Suitability:** Suitable for moderately bullish market conditions when the investor is willing to potentially sacrifice some downside protection for higher income potential.

In-the-Money (ITM) Covered Call

- **Benefits:** Offers strong downside protection due to the intrinsic value of the call option. Provides consistent income and enhanced downside risk management.

- **Drawbacks:** Lower premium income compared to out-of-the-money options. Limited potential for capital appreciation.

- **Suitability:** Suitable for more cautious investors in mildly bullish to neutral market conditions, prioritizing capital preservation and income.

Ratio Covered Call

- **Benefits:** Generates additional premium income by selling more call options than the number of shares owned. Allows for potential profits even if the stock price moves significantly.

- **Drawbacks:** Increased complexity and risk. Losses can be amplified if the stock price drops sharply.

- **Suitability:** Suitable for moderately bullish to neutral market conditions with a bullish bias. Requires a good understanding of options and higher risk tolerance.

Collar Strategy

- **Benefits:** Combines a covered call with a protective put. Provides downside protection while still generating income from the call premium.

- **Drawbacks:** Premiums from both sides of the trade might offset each other. Limits potential gains and income.

- **Suitability:** Suitable for uncertain or volatile market conditions when an investor seeks to hedge against potential losses while still generating some income.

Rolling Covered Call

- **Benefits:** Allows an investor to roll the call option to a later expiration date or a higher strike price, enhancing income potential and potentially capitalizing on changing market conditions.

- **Drawbacks:** Might result in missed capital gains if the stock price rises significantly before rolling.

- **Suitability:** Suitable for various market conditions. Requires active monitoring and decision-making skills to adapt to changing circumstances.

Dividend Capture Covered Call

- **Benefits:** Timed around the stock's ex-dividend date to capture both dividend income and call premium income.

- **Drawbacks:** Limited time window for implementation. Dividend capture might not fully offset potential losses if the stock price drops.

- **Suitability:** Suitable for investors looking to generate income from both dividends and options premiums. Requires careful timing and research.

Selecting the most suitable covered call strategy depends on your market outlook, risk tolerance, and investment goals. It's important to thoroughly understand the mechanics, benefits, and drawbacks of each strategy before implementation. Additionally, continuous market monitoring, risk management, and a well-defined exit plan are crucial components of successful covered call trading. If you're uncertain, seeking advice from experienced traders or financial professionals can help you make informed decisions that align with your financial goals. Selecting the right timing and strike price for covered calls is a crucial aspect of maximizing the effectiveness of this strategy. This decision involves considering factors such as market sentiment, potential capital gains, and the overall risk-reward profile. Here's a breakdown of how to approach these considerations:

Market Sentiment

Bullish Sentiment: If you're optimistic about the stock's prospects and expect it to rise or remain stable, you might lean towards writing covered calls with strike prices that are slightly higher than the current market price. This way, you can capture premium income while still benefiting from potential capital appreciation up to the strike price.

Neutral to Bearish Sentiment: If you're less bullish and expect the stock's price to remain relatively stagnant or even decrease, you might consider writing covered calls with strike prices closer to the current market price. This allows you to generate income while potentially benefiting from the stock's limited movement.

Potential Capital Gains

Lower Potential Gains: If the stock has a lower potential for significant capital gains, you might opt for slightly out-of-the-money covered calls. This way, you can capture additional income while aligning with the stock's more modest growth potential.

Higher Potential Gains: If you believe the stock has a higher potential for substantial capital gains, you might consider writing covered calls that are further out of the money. This allows you to benefit from the stock's upward movement while generating income.

Strike Price Selection:

In-the-Money (ITM) Calls: If you're more concerned about downside protection and prefer a conservative approach, you might choose in-the-money covered calls. These offer a greater level of protection due to the intrinsic value of the call option.

Out-of-the-Money (OTM) Calls: If you're comfortable with a moderate level of risk and want to enhance income potential, out-of-the-money covered calls might be suitable. These offer higher premium income but with less downside protection.

Time Horizon

Short-Term Calls: If you're focused on generating income over a short time frame, you might want to choose shorter-term covered calls. These provide more frequent premium income opportunities but require more active management.

Longer-Term Calls: If you're looking for a more consistent income stream over a longer period, longer-term covered calls could be preferable. These require less frequent adjustments and are better suited for a less hands-on approach.

Volatility

Higher Volatility: In a more volatile market environment, you might lean towards writing covered calls with higher strike prices. This allows you to capture more premium income from the increased volatility.

Lower Volatility: In a less volatile market, you might opt for covered calls with slightly lower strike prices. This enables you to generate income while accommodating the stock's potentially smaller price movements.

Remember that while these guidelines can help you make informed decisions, there's no one-size-fits-all approach to covered calls. Each investor's situation is unique, and it's important to thoroughly assess your risk tolerance, investment goals, and market outlook. Additionally, ongoing market monitoring and adjustments to your strategy are necessary to adapt to changing conditions. If you're unsure, consider seeking advice from experienced options traders or financial advisors to help you fine-tune your covered call strategy.

Protecting your positions through risk mitigation is a crucial aspect of successful options trading, including covered calls. Utilizing stop-loss orders, making adjustments, and diversifying your portfolio are key strategies to safeguard your investments. Here's how you can implement these risk mitigation techniques:

Utilizing Stop-Loss Orders

Stop-loss orders are tools that automatically trigger a market order to sell a position when a specified price is reached. While they are commonly associated with stock trading, they can also be employed in options trading, including covered calls.

- **Benefits:** Stop-loss orders can limit potential losses by exiting a position if the stock price drops beyond a certain threshold. This can provide peace of mind and prevent substantial losses.

- **Drawbacks:** In volatile markets, stop-loss orders can be triggered by short-term price fluctuations, resulting in selling at an unfavorable price.

- **Considerations:** Set your stop-loss level carefully, taking into account the stock's historical volatility and your risk tolerance. Avoid setting the stop-loss too close to the current price to prevent premature triggering.

Making Adjustments

Adjustments involve modifying your options position to adapt to changing market conditions and mitigate potential losses.

Rolling Options: If the stock price drops and your covered call position is at risk of being assigned, consider rolling the call option to a later expiration date or a lower strike price. This allows you to collect additional premium income and potentially recover from the loss.

Adding Protective Puts: In a covered call position, you can purchase protective put options on the same stock. This effectively creates a collar strategy, providing downside protection all while generating income from the covered call.

Diversifying Your Portfolio

Diversification involves spreading your investments across different stocks, sectors, or asset classes to reduce the impact of a single investment's poor performance.

- **Benefits:** Diversification minimizes the impact of a single stock's decline on your overall portfolio. It balances risk and potential returns.

- **Drawbacks:** Over-diversification might lead to diluted returns if one or more positions perform exceptionally well.

- **Considerations:** Diversify across various industries and sectors to ensure that your portfolio is not overly exposed to the risks of a specific market segment.

Continuous Monitoring and Learning

Stay actively engaged with your portfolio by regularly monitoring market conditions and news that might affect your positions. Staying informed helps you make timely adjustments and decisions.

- **Benefits:** Staying informed allows you to make educated decisions based on the most recent information, potentially minimizing losses and capitalizing on opportunities.

- **Drawbacks:** Neglecting to monitor your portfolio can lead to missed chances to adjust positions or react to changing market conditions.

- **Considerations:** Continuously educate yourself about options trading strategies, market trends, and economic indicators to make informed decisions.

Risk mitigation is an ongoing process that requires vigilance, discipline, and adaptation. Employing stop-loss orders, making adjustments, diversifying your portfolio, and staying informed are essential components of managing risk and protecting your investments while engaged in options trading, including covered calls. If you're uncertain, consider seeking guidance from experienced options traders or financial advisors to develop a risk management plan that aligns with your financial goals and risk tolerance.

Chapter 4

Implementing the Options Wheel Strategy

This chapter summarizes everything you've learned so far and will teach you how to put it into practice. You'll find a step-by-step guide on how to apply the Options Wheel Strategy in your trades and understand the significance of consistent monitoring throughout the process. You'll also find practical strategies for adjusting positions to accommodate changing market dynamics, as well as some considerations to give you a comprehensive view of its financial implications. Finally, you'll understand why you should maintain accurate records of your trades and learn how to create a systematic approach.

Applying the Options Wheel Strategy

Step 1: Choose Your Account Size

No matter how skilled of a trader you are, when it comes to the stock market, a portion of your success is always in the hands of chance. The market is unpredictable regardless of how often you observe trends and predictions and how many hours you spend researching. This means that you should never invest more than you're willing to lose in hopes of generating more money. Think about all your financial obligations and create a reasonable budget.

Step 2: Diversify Your Portfolio

Once you've decided the amount of money you wish to invest, don't put it all in options trading. Portfolio diversification is the process of spreading your investment budget across several asset classes and types of investment. This helps reduce the risk of losing your money and can lead to higher returns. Investments that span different sectors and move in opposite directions will allow you to yield the most benefits of diversification.

Say you invest your money in the hospitality and technology industries. If a crisis affects the hospitality industry while the technology sector experiences a boom, the returns from the latter will offset the losses you incurred. This applies to different investment instruments as well. If you don't get lucky with options, the money you invest elsewhere might offset the loss.

As a rule of thumb, a good balance in your investment portfolio would be 60% in index funds and the rest in options. You can split the remaining 40% between options and other investment instruments if you want to test things out first. That said, you need at least $2500 in your account to start with options. This way, you'll be able to trade on ETFs or stocks.

Step 3: Choose a Stock

The stock you choose to start with will dictate how well your account performs. Make sure to pick a stock you're positive will increase in value in the future. Besides selecting one that you're bullish on, you need to pick one that you can afford. Make a habit of choosing a stock that is 100x your account's value. For instance, if you choose one that trades for $50, you need to have $5000 in your account to start the wheel. Option contracts for decent stock and ETFs start at around $20, which is why you need at least $2500 to run the wheel.

Step 4: Sell a Cash-Covered Put

To sell a cash-secured put, you must have enough money to buy the shares of the underlying stock if you get assigned. Selling the put requires you to write a contract for someone else to buy. Buying the contract signals that you agree to buy 100 shares of the stock you selected if it falls under a strike price that you agree on. You get a premium in return for selling.

Example: You sold a put that expires by 8/3 and states that you'll agree to buy 100 shares of the stock you chose if its price drops below $300. The stock currently goes for $32o, which is why your contract requires $32,000 of collateral (320 x 100). If the stock doesn't go below $300 before the expiry date, the put will be worthless, and you can go into another one.

The premium that the buyer paid you is $1.6, which is $160 for all 100 shares. Even if the contract expires, you get to keep the premium as a profit. While you can keep earning your profit this way, you're going to make more money if you balance by either increasing the premium you receive or decreasing the strike price, depending on your risk tolerance. Lowering your strike price will lower your risk but will also result in a lower premium. If you choose to increase your strike price, you'll receive a higher premium, but will increase your risk.

You will find the right balance and understand your risk tolerance over time, but as a rule of thumb, a good premium should be at least 1% of the stock's price. You won't make significant profits if you accept anything lower than that.

Step 5: Repeat the Process Until Assignment

If the put you sold expired worthless, simply sell another put. Reflect on how you felt about the last put you sold and what you learned, and consider your risk tolerance to determine what you can fix this time. If the put expires again, it's great that you're making profits through premiums. Keep repeating and fine-tuning the process until the stock falls below your strike price and gets assigned.

Step 6: Sell a Covered Call

If the put you sold expired in-the-money and the buyer assigned, you will have to buy the 100 shares of stock. Take this situation as a learning experience and think about whether you took a substantial risk. Did you make profits with the premium? Evaluate this experience to determine what you can do better moving forward.

The 100 shares you're stuck with shouldn't feel like a burden if you choose the right stock. Hold it for a couple of weeks or even a few months until the stock's price increases before you sell a covered call.

You write a contract for someone else to buy, signaling that you agree to sell the shares you're holding if the stock rises above the strike price you decide. You'll receive a premium in return for the contract you sell.

Example: You agree to sell your shares by or before 22/6 if the stock rises above $340 and the buyer decides to exercise the contract. You'll receive a premium of $1.9, which totals $190 for 100 shares.

Step 5: Repeat

You should master the Options Wheel Strategy once you've gone through the cycle a few times. You'll make a profit every time a contract expires worthless or hold your shares before selling a covered call if it expires in-the-money.

Consistent Monitoring

Monitoring the process consistently when implementing the Options Wheel Strategy is crucial to your financial success.

Risk Management

The stock market is dynamic and highly volatile. Rapid fluctuations can happen unexpectedly. Monitoring the market regularly allows you to assess the effect of changing market conditions on your plan so you can adjust your positions accordingly. Staying attentive and alert will allow you to avoid potential dramatic losses and reduce your exposure to risks.

Market Insights

Monitoring the market conditions regularly gives you insights into new trends, notable events, and news that might affect the performance of the stocks you're interested in. Staying up-to-date on all the factors that might impact relevant industries allows you to make informed decisions regarding when to enter and exit positions.

Prompt Adjustments

If you notice that your market is moving against your position, you need to make timely adjustments to salvage the situation and avoid more losses. You can adjust your strategy by settling on new strike prices or adjusting your options contracts.

Increasing Returns

Monitoring your positions allows you to take advantage of any potential opportunities. This way, you can maximize the income you generate through premiums and rising stock values.

Mitigating Assignment Issues

You want to avoid situations where you're forced to buy or sell stock at certain prices or face risks associated with dividends, market fluctuations, or inadequate funds. Keeping a watchful eye keeps you prepared for potential assignments and allows you to come up with a clear strategy and stay updated with the brokerage rules. Knowledge and preparations can allow you to manage your assignments with ease, ensuring that they align with your trading strategy.

Strategies for Adjusting Positions

Rolling Options

- You should consider rolling up the put to a higher strike price if the price of the underlying stock increases rapidly. This way, you'll avoid assignment if the stock price approaches your initial strike price and receive a higher premium.

- You should roll down your strike price if the stock price falls significantly. This will allow you to mitigate potential assignment risks and lower your cost basis in case you're assigned.

- If you're selling a covered call and the stock's price rises, you should roll the call option up and increase your strike price. This way, you'll capitalize on the rising value of the stock.

Adjusting Strike Prices

If you're trading several options, you'll have spreads. Spreads are the differences in strike prices between the options contracts you're trading.

- Widening the spread or increasing the differences in strike prices between your long and short options can help you manage your risks more effectively and lower your likelihood of incurring losses.

- Narrowing your spreads can lead to higher profitability. However, you should only use this strategy when you're almost certain of the direction of the stock.

Changing Expiration Dates

- If you think that the market will take longer than anticipated to move in the direction you're hoping for, you can benefit from extending your contract's expiration date.

- If you make adjustments to your strategy and discover potential short-term opportunities, you can maximize your profits by shortening your contract's expiry date.

Adding or Reducing Contracts

- If you're generally optimistic about the trade you're conducting, start with a small and cautious position and gradually add more contracts if the market moves in the direction you want.

- If you have already achieved your profit target or feel like you're in a risky position, gradually reduce your contracts. This will allow you to avoid or cut losses or secure your profits.

Why You Should Maintain Accurate Records

- Maintaining accurate records of all your trades will allow you to evaluate your performance and assess your success rate over time. This way, you'll find out which approach and strategies work best for you, pinpoint areas in which you need improvement, and make informed decisions to maximize your returns.

- Keeping track of your trades allows you to minimize your exposure to risk. You can evaluate the capital you allocate and the size of your positions and calculate your risk-reward ratios to maintain a diversified portfolio.

- Maintaining accurate records is crucial for tax purposes. You should have clear indications of your entry and exit points, as well as your gains and losses to accurately report your tax at the end of the year.

- FOMO (fear of missing out) and biases are two things you should leave behind when you're exploring the stock market. Reviewing your past records will help you determine behavioral patterns and biases that impact your decisions.

How to Create a Systematic Approach

- Create a template in which you can keep accurate records of all your trades in a standardized format. For instance, you can create an Excel sheet that includes details like trade date, the strategy you implemented, underlying assets, entry and exit points, position size, and contract details.

- Trading journals, platforms, calendars, and other digital tools will make the trading process smoother. You can also subscribe to news outlets that are relevant to the industries you trade in to stay updated on all events that can influence the direction of the market.

- Update your records right after you execute a trade to avoid piling up the data and leaving out important details.

- Back-up your trade records in case you lose your data. Make sure all your copies are secure and only accessible to you.

Revisiting this step-by-step guide will help you navigate your trades with ease. Make sure to diversify your portfolio to manage your risks effectively and avoid incurring significant losses. Consistent monitoring, accurate record-keeping, and making strategic adjustments will help you maximize your profits and mitigate risks. The tips and strategies offered in this chapter will streamline your trades and allow you to implement the Options Wheel Strategy with confidence.

Chapter 5:

Advanced Techniques and Considerations

This chapter explores more complex strategies that can be applied alongside the Options Wheel. You'll understand how these strategies can help you increase your income potential while enhancing risk management and learn about the pros and cons of each. You'll find practical examples that will allow you to grasp the concepts effectively. You'll also find out why emotional discipline and rational decision-making are crucial to your success and understand how the Options Wheel can be a cornerstone of retirement planning and portfolio growth.

Collar Options Strategy

Implementing a collar options strategy can limit your risks while generating more income because it involves buying a protective put option and selling a covered collar. The main objective behind this strategy is to "collar" the underlying asset's value and keep it within a specific scope. This way, you can reduce the possibility of incurring significant losses during market downturns and lower hedging costs while taking on more opportunities for potential returns.

This common hedging technique requires you to hold a long position on the option's underlying assets. While this means that you'll only receive returns if the value of the asset rises, you will be exposed to significant losses if the value of the asset dramatically decreases. A protective put, which involves being bullish for an out-of-the-money option and holding a long position in it, can allow you to mitigate this risk. A protective put is set at a floor price, which is the maximum number of losses you can incur even if the asset's value falls further. This additional level of protection, however, requires a premium.

Selling a covered call allows you to recover the cost of the premium you paid by generating profit from another. You must keep in mind, however, that this strategy limits your gains in the same way that it limits your profits. You would only earn returns up to the strike price, even if the asset's value exceeded that level. The call and put options' strike prices serve as the range of your returns.

Buying a call option signals that you're betting that the underlying asset's price will rise above the strike price. When this happens, you will gain from the asset's appreciation. However, if the asset's price doesn't rise enough to cover the premium for the call option, you might incur a loss equal to the amount you pay.

You buy a put option when you are certain the cost of the underlying asset will be less than the strike price. If this happens, you'll obtain returns from the asset's depreciation. If it doesn't fall enough to cover the premium, you'll incur a loss equivalent to that amount.

Your gains and losses are largely influenced by the premiums you pay and the price movement of the asset. If the price doesn't move in the direction you desire, your returns will be offset by the cost of the premium. The success of this strategy not only requires you to forecast the direction in which the price of the underlying asset will move but also to consider the extent of the movement.

Example 1

Say the market price of an asset that you hold a long position in is $100. You're positive that you're going to generate returns in the long run but aren't sure about the short-term gains. You then buy a put option with a $88 strike price at a $5 premium. You also sell a call option for $5 at a $110 strike price. The asset's price appreciated to $108 around a week later.

You will lose $5 from the put option premium and gain $5 from that of the call option since the underlying asset's price increased by $8.

Example 2

Say you're holding a long position in a stock that currently trades at $120. You buy a put option for $3 with a $110 strike price and sell a call option for $4 with a $13o strike price.

- If the stock's price falls below $110, the protective put will still allow you to sell the stock at $110.

- You'll keep the profits you generated from the premiums you collected from the call and put options if the stock's price remains between $110 and $130.

- If the stock's price rises above $130, you'll have to sell the stock at only $130 with a covered call.

Advantages

- The collar strategy is a very effective risk-hedging technique and is especially beneficial if you're investing a large sum of money.

- This is a strategy that allows you to offset potential losses is crucial since the stock market is characterized by its volatility.

- Since a protective put is enough to help you mitigate losses, you must sell a call option to cover the cost of the premium you paid.

- You might generate more income by holding an underlying asset because you're eligible to receive dividend payments.

Disadvantages

- It might be unappealing because it limits the profits you can receive. It limits your losses by limiting your gains.

- It can be very complex to grasp and effectively apply at first.

- Others may benefit if the underlying asset's price rises above the strike price of the call option.

Options Spread Strategies

Options spread strategies use several options within one asset class and they tend to be set at various strike prices and expiration dates. The variety of strike prices and expiration dates lead to spread positions. Spreads allow investors to make the best of the differences between various option prices. Traders can come up with positions that allow them to capitalize on the variations in their options, which increases profits and lowers risk.

The three primary types of option spreads are:

1. **Horizontal spreads:** This is the type of spread that takes place when options with the same underlying assets have the same strike prices but different expiration dates.

2. **Vertical spreads:** This type of spread includes options with different strike prices but similar underlying assets and expiration dates.

3. **Diagonal spreads:** These spreads have identical underlying securities. However, their expiration dates and strike prices may vary.

Example 1 - Call Spread

Say the stock's market price is $163, and you have 100 shares in your options contract, which expires in a month. You sell a call for $2 with a $165 strike price and simultaneously buy another one at $1 with a $180 strike price. The net entry price, or net premium would be $1 ($2 - $1). The maximum potential profit is $100 and is calculated by multiplying the net premium by the number of shares ($1 x 100).

In this example, the call spread is $15 ($180 - $165). To calculate the maximum potential loss, you would subtract the net premium from the call spread ($15 - $1) and multiply it by the number of shares ($14 x 100). If the trade doesn't go as you had hoped and the stock price moves against your position, you can lose up to $1400.

Example 2 - Put Spread

Say the stock's market price is $330, and you have 100 shares in your options contract, which expires in a month. You sell a put for $5.60 with a $315 strike price and simultaneously buy another one at $4.45 with a $310 strike price. The net entry price would be $1.15 ($5.60 - $4.45).

The maximum potential profit is $115 ($1.15 x 100), which is the maximum profit you can make if the stock price moves toward your position. In this example, the put spread is $5 ($315 - $310). The loss you'll incur if the stock price moves against your position is up to $385 ($5 - $1.15) x 100).

Debit and Credit Spreads

- Debit and credit spreads are options trading strategies used to generate profit based on the premiums of the traded options.

- If you sell an option for a higher premium than the premium of the option you bought, you'll receive credit when you enter the spread, creating a credit spread.

- Conversely, entering the spread on a debit means that the premium of the option sold is lower than that of the option bought, creating a debit spread.

Spread Combinations

- These are considered complex options strategies that allow you to reduce your risk exposure while generating profit.

- A box spread is an example of a spread combination that involves pairing a bear put spread with a bull call spread.

- Spread combinations are usually employed when you're expecting the underlying stock to experience limited price movements. In that case, the premium you paid is your maximum loss.

Advantages

- Options spread strategies help you limit your exposure to risk by hedging your position.

- They make you eligible to receive dividend payments by investing in underlying assets while trading on your position.

- You have a high opportunity to earn profit even though you can limit your risk exposure while investing.

Disadvantages

- Implementing this strategy can be tricky for beginners because it requires expertise and a certain level of trading mastery.

- Like all investment and trading instruments, there's a trade-off between limited risk and high profits.

- Many investors believe that the risk-to-reward ratio is insignificant. While the risk is relatively limited, it's still relatively high compared to the profit you earn.

The Benefits of Implementing These Techniques

Collar Strategy

- **Risk Management**

Implementing a collar strategy can help you with risk management as it serves as a means of insurance in case the stock price drops, leading to potentially significant losses. Your put option's value will appreciate if the stock falls, offsetting your loss. The call option you sell will generate income, offsetting the premium you paid to buy the put option and lowering your net cost.

- **Income Potential**

You'll generate premium income by selling the call option. This can be a source of additional profit or can be used to cover the premium you paid for the put option. You can also yield returns from selling the call option.

Spread Strategies

- **Risk Management**

Implementing credit spreads requires you to sell an option with a higher premium than that you bought the option for. The premium you received in return for selling offsets the premium you paid for buying the option, reducing your position's cost and limiting your losses.

Implementing debit spreads requires you to buy an option with a higher premium than that you sold for. While you would be incurring a debit, it limits your potential losses by lowering the amount of money you have at risk.

- **Income Potential**

Credit spreads offer immediate income because they involve an upfront net premium payment. You'll be able to keep the entire premium as profit if the options expire out-of-the-money.

Debit spreads allow you to generate profit from the difference in both premiums as the options move toward expiration and the spread narrows or closes in your direction.

Emotional Discipline and Rational Decision-Making

- Fear and greed can push you to make impulsive decisions, which can lead to dramatic losses. Practicing emotional decisions will allow you to stick to your goals and strategies and take calculated risks.

- Emotional trading can cause you to conduct unnecessary trades, increasing your risk exposure and transaction costs.

- Avoiding emotional decisions allows you to perform thorough analyses and come up with rational strategies to follow through with.

- Emotional discipline allows you to assess risks objectively and determine reasonable position sizes.

- The stock market is highly volatile, which can lead to stress and anxiety. Maintaining emotional discipline will allow you to stay calm and make rational decisions.

Retirement Planning and Portfolio Growth

The Options Wheel Strategy is a cornerstone of portfolio management and can help with retirement planning due to its high potential for income generation and risk management elements.

The Options Wheel Strategy will:

- Lead to steady income generation.

- Allow you to acquire quality assets and stock at discounted prices.

- Offer downside protection, allowing you to mitigate risk and protect your portfolio.

- Be easily applied to various stocks, further diversifying your portfolio.

- Align well with retirement planning as it encourages a long-term investment approach.

Investors use both collar and spread strategies to manage their risks and generate income while trading options. They are designed to maintain a balance between risk exposure and profit generation, depending on the investor's goals and market outlook. Emotional discipline and rational decision-making are crucial to investment and financial success because they ensure you effectively and consistently apply your strategies.

Conclusion

Now that you've finished this book, it's up to you to use all the knowledge you've acquired. The insights, information, and practical strategies you've learned can reshape your future and help you achieve your goals. This quick yet enlightening read has illustrated the world of possibilities that options trading presents. You now understand that diversifying your income portfolio and unlocking passive revenue streams is not a fantasy but a viable reality.

There will be times when you feel overwhelmed and lost in the sea of options trading. Don't let that discourage you. Revisit the concepts explored in this book whenever you need guidance to refine your strategy, make informed decisions, and seize the opportunities that come your way. Always remember that practicing emotional discipline, making rational decisions, and properly assessing and managing the risks involved are just as important as applying strategies and techniques.

This is more than just a guide. It is an empowering toolkit. It teaches you how each choice and opportunity you have plays a significant role in shaping your financial journey. Reflect on how you can apply your knowledge to enhance your risk management, increase your income growth potential, and tailor your approach to align with your goals. The Options Wheel strategy can drive you toward financial success, whether you wish to plan for retirement or grow your portfolio.

Whether you're a beginner or a seasoned investor, continuous learning and development is the key to financial transformation and success. Growing your knowledge will allow you to easily navigate unknown situations and explore fresh perspectives when needed. Remember that your journey toward financial freedom is ongoing, and this book is a step in the right direction. Reading it has given you the enlightenment and motivation to work toward your monetary aspirations, but you will pave the way to achieve them.

<h1 style="text-align: center;">References</h1>

(N.d.). Nasdaq.com. https://www.nasdaq.com/articles/everything-you-need-to-know-about-cash-secured-puts

(N.d.). Nasdaq.com. https://www.nasdaq.com/articles/how-adjust-your-covered-calls-fly-maximum-profits-2014-01-22

Adams, J. (2022). Retirement Planning and Goals Options Wheel Strategy – Follow-Up. Easy Investing Income. https://easyinvestingincome.com/retirement-planning-and-goals-options-wheel-strategy-follow-up/

Cash-Secured Put. (n.d.). https://www.optionseducation.org/strategies/all-strategies/cash-secured-put

Coglianese, J. (2020). Why Trade Spread Options? StoneX Financial Inc, Daniels Trading Division. https://www.danielstrading.com/2011/07/16/why-trade-spread-options

Collar Strategy In Options Trading - Examples, Pros & Cons | Investology | Nuvama. (n.d.). Nuvama. https://www.nuvamawealth.com/investology/introduction-to-derivative-markets-8335c5/collar-strategy-in-options-trading-95298b

Crawley, P. (2023). The Options Wheel Strategy: Wheel Trade Explained. SteadyOptions. https://steadyoptions.com/articles/the-options-wheel-strategy-wheel-trade-explained-r632/

Crawley, P. (2023). The Options Wheel Strategy: Wheel Trade Explained. SteadyOptions. https://steadyoptions.com/articles/the-options-wheel-strategy-wheel-trade-explained-r632/

Exchange, M. (2019, September 6). Covered calls: Managing risk exposure and generating value during volatile times. Option Matters. https://www.optionmatters.ca/covered-calls-managing-risk-exposure-and-generating-value-during-volatile-times/

Gad, S. (2010, August 23). How to sell put options to benefit in any market. Investopedia. https://www.investopedia.com/articles/optioninvestor/10/sell-puts-benefit-any-market.asp

Ganti, A. (2003, November 19). Covered calls: How they work and how to use them in investing. Investopedia. https://www.investopedia.com/terms/c/covered-call.asp

Ganti, A. (2022). Covered Calls: How They Work and How to Use Them in Investing. Investopedia. https://www.investopedia.com/terms/c/coveredcall.asp

Gavin. (2022, June 24). The Ultimate Guide to the Wheel Options Strategy. Options Trading IQ. https://optionstradingiq.com/options-wheel-strategy/

How to Trade the Options Wheel Strategy | Option Alpha Guide. (2022, July 8). https://optionalpha.com/blog/wheel-strategy

Jackson, A. (2023, April 28). Options Trading – A Beginner's Guide On How To Trade Options. Forbes Advisor INDIA. https://www.forbes.com/advisor/in/investing/options-trading/

James Royal, Ph.D. (2023). Why is portfolio diversification important for investors? Bankrate. https://www.bankrate.com/investing/diversification-is-important-in-investing/#develop

Kulkarni, V. (2023, March 25). Cash Secured Puts- How It Works, Benefits and limitations. Wint Wealth. https://www.wintwealth.com/blog/cash-secured-puts-how-it-works-benefits-and-limitations/

Monitoring Trades - Assessing Performance to Improve. (n.d.). https://www.optionstrading.org/getting-started/monitoring-trades/

Nielsen, J. (2023, February 28). How to use A cash-secured put option strategy. Investor's Business Daily. https://www.investors.com/research/options/cash-secured-how-to-use-this-options-strategy/

O'Brien, T. (2023, May 24). Trading Psychology: Mastering Your Emotions in Binary Options Trading - Galway Daily. Galway Daily. https://www.galwaydaily.com/more/trading-psychology-mastering-your-emotions-in-binary-options-trading/

Ramachandran, A. (2023). Options Spread. WallStreetMojo. https://www.wallstreetmojo.com/options-spread/

Team, W. (2023). Collar Options Strategy. WallStreetMojo. https://www.wallstreetmojo.com/collar-options-strategy/

The Wheel Strategy in Options Trading: A Complete Guide | TOP1 Markets. (n.d.). https://www.top1markets.com/insights/The-Wheel-Strategy-in-Options-Trading-A-Complete-Guide

Theta, P. (2022, August 16). The Wheel Options Strategy for Beginners | Mastering Options. Medium. https://medium.com/mastering-options/how-to-use-the-options-wheel-strategy-5013c9938f4b

Thompson, C. (2023). Trading Psychology: What it is and Importance. Investopedia. https://www.investopedia.com/articles/trading/02/110502.asp

Toney-Hoffman, M. (2023, August 21). The Wheel Strategy Explained | 3 Things You Must Know. Financial Tech Wiz. https://www.financialtechwiz.com/post/wheel-options-strategy

Using the Probability Calculator. (2018, April 5). [Video]. https://www.fidelity.com/viewpoints/active-investor/hitting-the-right-strike-price

What Is Options Trading and How to Trade Options? (n.d.). https://www.moomoo.com/us/learn/detail-what-is-options-trading-and-how-to-trade-options-83531-221183101

Wheel Strategy Tips: When To Exit Trades | Linke-dIn. (2022, April 22). https://www.linkedin.com/pulse/wheel-strategy-tips-when-exit-trades-markus-heit-koetter/

Yegge, M. (1683918209000). The top covered call strat-egies for maximizing your passive income. Linke-din.com. https://www.linkedin.com/pulse/top-cov-ered-call-strategies-maximizing-your-passive-in-come-mark-yegge

www.ingramcontent.com/pod-product-compliance
Lightning Source LLC
Chambersburg PA
CBHW050600160726
48003CB00002B/975